Inventors and Creators

Stan Lee

Creator of Spider-Man

Raymond H. Miller

KIDHAVEN PRESS

An imprint of Thomson Gale, a part of The Thomson Corporation

THOMSON

™

GALE

Detroit • New York • San Francisco • San Diego • New Haven, Conn. • Waterville, Maine • London • Munich

J
921
LEE

LIBRARY OF CONGRESS CATALOGING-IN-PUBLICATION DATA

Miller, Raymond H., 1967–
  Stan Lee / By Raymond H. Miller.
    p. cm. -- (Inventors and creators)
  Includes bibliographical references and index.
  ISBN 0-7377-3447-7 (alk. paper)
  1. Lee, Stan—Juvenile literature. 2. Cartoonists—United States—Biography—
Juvenile literature. I. Title. II. Series.
  PN6727.L39Z79 2006
  741.4092--dc22   2005026845

Printed in the United States of America

Contents

Chapter One

Stanley Lieber

Stan Lee was born Stanley Martin Lieber on December 28, 1922, in New York City. He was the oldest of Jack and Celia Lieber's two sons. His brother, Larry, was born nine years later. Stanley's parents were Jewish Romanian **immigrants**. They were among the many thousands of people who had moved to the United States in the early 1900s, hoping to find a better way of life.

For the Liebers, however, life remained a struggle. Jack worked long hours for little pay as a dress cutter in New York's garment district, while Celia took care of Stanley and tended to the family's home. Things went from bad to worse when the **Great Depression** hit the nation in 1929, causing widespread unemployment. Jack was soon out of work. He searched the city for a new job, but found that no one was hiring. "I always felt sorry for my father," Stanley later recalled. "He was a good man, honest and caring. He wanted the best for his family, as most parents do. But the times were against him. At the height of the Depression, there were just no jobs to be had."[1]

Spider-Man creator Stan Lee, whose original name was Stanley Lieber, relaxes in his Los Angeles office in this 2005 photo.

To save money, the Liebers moved into a tiny, run-down apartment in the Bronx, a **borough** of New York City that was home to many Jewish immigrants. Stanley knew that he and his family had nowhere else to go. Still, he hated the apartment. A back alley wall blocked his view when he looked out the window, and the apartment was so tiny that the living room doubled as his bedroom. He spent most of his time playing outdoors with his friends.

Finding an Escape

As the Depression stretched well into the 1930s, life became even more difficult for the Lieber family. Jack invested money from the family's savings in a restaurant,

As a young boy, Stanley enjoyed the works of English playwright William Shakespeare.

but the business eventually failed. The lack of money led to frequent arguments between Jack and Celia, which was hard on Stanley and Larry. Already a strict father, Jack became even more demanding with his sons the longer he remained at home without a job. Celia tried to balance her husband's strict ways by treating Stanley and Larry with love and tenderness. As a result, the two boys developed a close bond with their mother.

Stanley found an escape from his demanding father and the difficult times by reading. He read everything from cereal boxes to novels. He especially loved exploring the works of the great **playwright** William Shakespeare, which he started reading before the age of ten. Not everything Stanley read was so serious, though. He enjoyed reading newspaper comic strips every day.

Stanley also loved watching movies. He sometimes walked to the local movie theater when he could find the twenty-five cents it took to buy a ticket. He preferred movies that were packed with adventure and drama. His favorite actors of the day were Errol Flynn and Roy Rogers.

No matter how difficult things were during the Depression, however, Stanley always looked forward to Saturday night, which was set aside for family night at the Lieber home. Everyone gathered around the radio and listened to Fred Allen and Jack Benny, popular comedians of the early broadcast era. Stanley was developing a taste for entertainment.

School Days

In school, Stanley also loved to be entertained. His favorite teacher, Mr. Ginsberg, began each class by telling the students a funny story. Stanley always looked forward to those stories. He later recalled the impact his teacher had on him: "Mr. Ginsberg taught me a really great lesson, and it's one I've tried to follow all my life: Whenever I want to communicate to others, I always try to do it in a lighter-hearted way and make it as entertaining as possible."[2]

While attending DeWitt Clinton High School, Stanley participated in many of the school's clubs, including the chess club, the French club, the law society, the Ping-Pong club, and the public-speaking club. He also worked on the school's student literary magazine, called the *Magpie*, where he served as publicity director. Even though Stanley did not write for the *Magpie*, he enjoyed writing articles in his spare time. At the age of fifteen he entered a weekly writing contest called "The Biggest News of the Week" and won three weeks in a row. The editor asked Stanley to stop submitting articles for the contest so others would have a chance to win. "I don't remember the editor's name, but his suggestion probably changed my life. He advised me to think about becoming a professional writer,"[3] Stanley said later.

Besides being a gifted writer, Stanley had a knack for making people laugh. One day he arrived in class early and found a ladder that had been left by a painter. He quickly climbed the ladder and jokingly wrote the words "Stan Lee is God" on the ceiling. It was the first known use of the name by which the world would later know him. In his senior yearbook he wrote that his life's ambition was to "Reach the Top— And STAY There." He also said he wanted to "join the

Stanley participated in the chess club, the Ping-Pong club, and several other clubs as a student in high school.

Navy, so the world can see me!"[4] Stanley graduated from high school in 1939.

A Timely Opportunity

If Stanley was ever to reach the top, he would have to do so without a college education. His parents needed him to go to work immediately after graduation so that he could help support the family. He worked for several low-paying employers, including a trouser manufacturer. There, he served as an errand boy for a company salesman. He felt humiliated every time the man yelled, "Boy!" and ordered him to fetch something. Stanley was relieved when he was fired after only two weeks on the job.

Stan Lee has always enjoyed making people laugh.

Unemployed at age seventeen, Stanley began to think about a career in writing. His uncle worked at Timely Publications, a comic book company, and told him about an opening there. Stanley enjoyed comics, but he doubted anyone would hire him without any experience. Fortunately for Stanley, the owner of Timely Publications was Martin Goodman, who was married to one of Stanley's cousins. Through this connection, Stanley received an interview with Joe Simon, the company's editor, in 1940. Simon introduced Stanley to Jack Kirby, the company's art director. Stanley was offered a job as Simon's personal assistant. Although the job did not pay much—only eight dollars a week—Stanley accepted. He did not know what the future held for him at Timely Publications, but he hoped that he might one day be able to write stories for the next great comic book.

Chapter Two

Stanley Becomes Stan Lee

At the time Stanley started working at Timely Publications, the company employed just seven people, most of whom were relatives of Martin Goodman's. As an assistant to Joe Simon, Stanley did everything from sweep the floors to keep the ink bottles full. But he also got to clean up the artwork by erasing stray pencil marks before it was sent to print, which he loved doing. In his spare time, he annoyed his coworkers by playing tunes such as "Yankee Doodle" on his **recorder**. Stanley was having the time of his life.

It was the perfect time for a young man like Stanley to catch on with a comic book company and make his mark. The comic book craze had started just a few years earlier when a new company called Detective Comics, later known as DC Comics, published *Action Comics #1*. The comic book introduced a caped superhero known as Superman. The public had never seen anything like Superman, and by 1939, DC was selling more than a million copies a month. Martin Goodman knew that he had to develop his own line of superhero comic books if his company was ever to compete

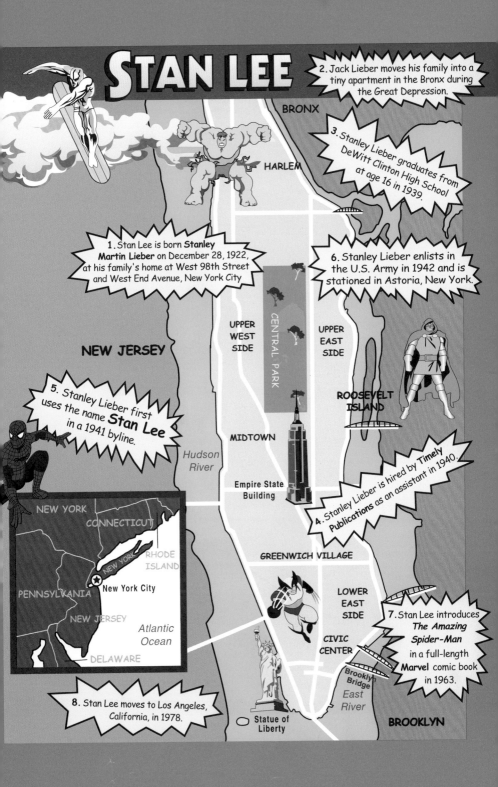

STAN LEE

1. Stan Lee is born **Stanley Martin Lieber** on December 28, 1922, at his family's home at West 98th Street and West End Avenue, New York City

2. Jack Lieber moves his family into a tiny apartment in the Bronx during the Great Depression.

3. Stanley Lieber graduates from DeWitt Clinton High School at age 16 in 1939.

4. Stanley Lieber is hired by Timely Publications as an assistant in 1940.

5. Stanley Lieber first uses the name **Stan Lee** in a 1941 byline.

6. Stanley Lieber enlists in the U.S. Army in 1942 and is stationed in Astoria, New York.

7. Stan Lee introduces *The Amazing Spider-Man* in a full-length **Marvel** comic book in 1963.

8. Stan Lee moves to Los Angeles, California, in 1978.

BRONX

HARLEM

NEW JERSEY

UPPER WEST SIDE

CENTRAL PARK

UPPER EAST SIDE

ROOSEVELT ISLAND

MIDTOWN

Hudson River

Empire State Building

GREENWICH VILLAGE

LOWER EAST SIDE

CIVIC CENTER

Brooklyn Bridge

East River

BROOKLYN

Statue of Liberty

NEW YORK

CONNECTICUT

RHODE ISLAND

NEW YORK

New York City

PENNSYLVANIA

NEW JERSEY

Atlantic Ocean

DELAWARE

Stan Lee did not create Captain America, but he did write some of the first stories featuring the character.

against DC. In late 1940, he introduced the red, white, and blue–costumed character Captain America.

Traitor's Revenge

Before his first week at Timely had ended, Stanley bragged that he already knew everything and was ready for a promotion. Simon soon thought of a job that might be ideal for his ambitious assistant. In the early days of comic books, publishers included two-page inserts called "text fillers" in order to qualify for cheaper mailing rates. Simon assigned Stanley to write one of the stories. The fillers had no pictures and were unrelated to the main story in the book. Still, Stanley was thrilled about the opportunity.

Stanley quickly turned in a piece twenty-six paragraphs long called "Captain America Foils the Traitor's Revenge." Although critics largely agree the story was not very well written, it featured a key theme Stanley would later use to great effect—the secret of the superhero's true identity. The story is set at night in a U.S. Army camp, where three would-be assassins are defeated by Captain America and his sidekick, Bucky. The next day, Private Steve Rogers, whose secret identity is Captain America, is yelled at by the camp colonel for sleeping through the excitement. "Captain America and Bucky mopped up three armed men by themselves and saved my life—and YOU were asleep!" wrote Stanley in the story. "Oh, why can't I have some soldiers like Captain America in this army—instead of YOU!"[5]

"Traitor's Revenge" appeared in the third issue of *Captain America Comics*, which appeared on newsstands in May 1941. Stanley was thrilled to be published for the first time, but the story was significant for another reason as well. For the byline, Stanley decided to split his first name in two, dropping the "y" at the end and adding an "e." With a stroke of the pen, Stanley Lieber became known as Stan Lee. The reason for the name change, he later recalled, was "because I felt someday I'd be writing the Great American Novel and I didn't want to use my real name on these silly little comics."[6]

On-the-Job Training

It was not long before Stan Lee was offered his first comic book script. He called it "Headline Hunter, Foreign Correspondent." It appeared in *Captain America Comics* #5, which went on sale in August 1941 and ran for eight issues. The "Headline Hunter" story opened with a large panel that read, "Story by Stan Lee." In those days, the authors of comics were rarely credited. Most comic book writers wanted only to be paid for the work they produced and cared little about recognition. Stan Lee was not one of those writers. Even though he planned one day to write novels for adults, he also wanted to make a name for himself in the comic book industry.

When Simon and Kirby were fired for secretly submitting work to DC Comics, most of the editorial duties went to Lee. Goodman eventually made him editor at Timely, but only on a temporary basis. Goodman hoped to find an older, more experienced writer to fill the position permanently. After all, Lee was just nineteen years old. Even so, he believed he was ready

Although he never intended to write comic books, Stan Lee became one of the most celebrated comic book authors of all time.

for the job. He was given his own office, where he penned the scripts for *Captain America Comics* and other comics that featured lesser-known superheroes, such as the Whizzer and Black Marvel.

Forced to learn on the job, Lee worked hard to improve. He read comics by established professionals and tried to refine some of their techniques. For example, he picked up dialogue tips from Batman writer Bill Finger. Eventually, Lee became more comfortable as a writer and his work began to improve. He became known for using dialogue that pushed the action to its limit. As for plots, he tried to keep them simple. "I'd have a plot in my mind," he recalls, "always the simplest plot in the world, and I'd start writing. I'd try to think, what would the first panel be? Then I'd write a description of what the picture should be, then I'd think, what should the characters say? Or what caption do I want to write? Then I'd go on to panel two, and I'd keep doing it until I reached page ten, the end."[7]

Military Man

Just as Lee was finding success in the comic book business, his career was interrupted by war. After Japan drew the United States into World War II with its surprise attack on Pearl Harbor, a patriotic Lee was eager to sign up to help in the war effort. On November 9, 1942, he enlisted in the army and was assigned to the communications division. Initially, Lee's military career did not take him far from home. He was stationed in Astoria in the borough of Queens. He later went to posts in North Carolina and Indiana.

Lee's brief time as a comic book writer served him well in the army. One of his main tasks was writing and illustrating training manuals for all of the branches of the military. He attempted to incorporate the energy and lighthearted fun that had become traits in his comic book stories. For a payroll training manual, he developed a character named Fiscal Freddy. Though Lee kept busy writing manuals during the day, he still found time in the evenings and on weekends to write for Timely. One of his tales, called "Super Soldier," which appeared in *Krazy Komics #15*, was signed "Pfc. Stan Lee."

The abbreviation stood for private first class, his army rank.

After almost three years in the service, Lee received an honorable discharge. His discharge paper listed him as playwright, one of fewer than ten people in U.S. history to be so named by the military. After leaving the service, Lee returned to his job at Timely.

Stan Lee joined the army less than a year after the Japanese attack on Pearl Harbor (pictured) drew the United States into World War II.

Comic Books Lose Popularity

A few years later, at a function for Timely, he met a model from England named Joan Boocock. The pair dated for just two weeks before getting married. Three years after that, they had a daughter, whom they named Joan Celia. Three years later, in 1953, tragedy struck when a second daughter died a few days after birth. Stan and Joan were heartbroken.

Making matters worse for Lee, comic books were beginning to fade in popularity. By 1955 Timely Publications, which had changed its name to Atlas Comics, had cancelled *Sub-Mariner*, the last of its superhero

Joan and Stan Lee have been married for more than fifty years.

comics. Two years later Atlas Comics collapsed after a work stoppage, but Lee kept his job, working for Goodman in magazine management, another division of the company. He began writing monster stories for a monthly magazine called *Tales to Astonish*. He also wrote stories for the company's romance and western comic books.

As Lee approached age 40, he began to think he was getting too old to turn out comic books day after day. Besides, he was afraid he would never be taken seriously as a writer. He was ready to quit his job and pursue other writing opportunities.

Chapter Three

Spider-Mania

In the late 1950s, with Lee's future in comic books in doubt, he started his own publishing company, Madison Publications. The first two titles he wrote under the Madison imprint were books of humor, *Blushing Burbs* and *Golfers Anonymous*. In both books, Lee wrote funny quotes and inserted them next to photographs of people. He sold ten thousand copies of each title.

Lee enjoyed writing humor so much that he penned a similar book called *You Don't Say!* This book was a bit more sophisticated than his first two. It featured photos of national and political leaders with satirical captions. His *Monster Madness* and *Monsters to Laugh With* featured still shots of B-movie monsters alongside Lee's witty phrases. "I loved doing them," Lee writes in his autobiography. "I think they helped me get over the blues at a time when I felt my day job was becoming more and more of a dead end."[8]

In the meantime, superhero comic books had started to make a comeback, and Atlas Comics was back in business. Martin Goodman turned to his star writer to

Stan Lee wrote several humorous books for his own imprint, Madison Publications.

develop a comic featuring a superhero group to rival DC's Justice League of America. But Lee was content to continue writing humor. It took some convincing from his wife, Joan, to return to writing superhero comic books for Atlas.

Excelsior!

For Lee's first attempt, he teamed up with Jack Kirby, who had been rehired, to create a new group of superheroes: The Fantastic Four. The tale involved four seemingly ordinary people, Reed Richards and his fiancée, Susan Storm; Susan's brother, Johnny Storm; and Ben Grimm. Lee wrote the story in the early years of the space race between the United States and the Soviet Union, and he based the origins of the superheroes on those events. In the story, Reed designs a rocket ship in hopes of beating the Soviets into space. He and the others are bound for space when a mysterious green cosmic ray knocks the spacecraft out of the sky. All four survive the crash and learn that the green ray has given them unique powers. Reed can stretch his body like rubber, Susan can make herself disappear, Johnny is able to burst into flames and fly through the sky, and Ben has the ability to turn into a large monster with rocklike skin and super strength. They rename themselves Mr. Fantastic, the Invisible Girl, the Human Torch, and the Thing.

The Fantastic Four #1 hit newsstands in November 1961. With Lee's snappy dialogue and Kirby's colorful characters, the comic book became an instant success. "A good comic book story has what

The Fantastic Four, which included the Human Torch, were a new group of superheroes created by Stan Lee and Jack Kirby.

any good adventure story has, except it's illustrated," Lee reveals. "That's all. But it has to have all the elements, good characterization, believable dialog and exciting situations that make you want to go to the next page."[9]

Lee wanted to capitalize on the popularity of the new comic and quickly began writing follow-up stories. He also expanded the Atlas Comics superhero line to include the Incredible Hulk, followed by the Mighty Thor and Iron Man. In addition to writing exciting stories, Lee made innovative changes to the comic book industry. He became the first editor to include a commentary page on which he answered fans' questions and gave hints about plots in future stories. "Stan's Soapbox" gave readers a chance to see Lee at his best. He sprinkled his commentary with fun words and phrases, such as "Face Front, True Believers!" "Nuff Said!" and "Excelsior!" which means "ever upward." "Excelsior!" became his signature motto.

With Great Power Comes Great Responsibility

In May 1963, Martin Goodman's comic book company officially became known as Marvel Comics, and

Stan Lee created the Incredible Hulk in 1962. A computer-generated version of the character was used in the 2003 *Hulk* movie.

Lee was its most important and busiest employee. As editor he handled the bulk of the writing duties. With four new superhero comic books due in newsstands each month, he and artist Jack Kirby worked frantically to complete the stories and artwork on time. Despite his hectic schedule, Lee was thrilled that the public had embraced the Marvel line of superhero comics. He had finally become comfortable with the fame that came with being a successful comic book writer. His best work, however, was yet to come.

Lee's next contribution occurred with an eleven-page original story for Marvel's *Amazing Fantasy #15*. Lee teamed with longtime Goodman artist Steve Ditko to create Spider-Man. Lee explains how he came up with the idea for his most famous creation: "The thing with the superhero that you have to get is a unique superpower. . . .We already had somebody who was the strongest guy in the world, somebody who could fly, and so forth. I thought what else is left? Then . . . I saw a fly crawling on the wall. And I said, wow, suppose a person had the power to stick to a wall like an insect. So I was off and running. And I thought, what will I call him? I tried Mosquito-Man, that didn't have any glamour, Insect-Man, that was even worse. I went down the line . . . and I got to Spider-Man. It sounded mysterious and dramatic, and, lo, a legend was born."[10]

In the story, a teenager named Peter Parker attends a science exhibit and is bitten by a radioactive spider that has dangled in front of a laser beam. The venom enters Parker's bloodstream and gives him the relative strength of a spider. But before he can use his new powers for good, tragedy strikes. His beloved Uncle Ben is killed by a robber Parker had refused to stop earlier that day. The grief-stricken teenager vows never again to pass up the chance to confront evil in the world. Lee's story ends with the words, "With great power there must also come great responsibility." This became Spider-Man's motto.

The Marvel Age of Comics

Lee was thrilled when the public quickly embraced his web-swinging superhero and demanded more stories. He went to work on a full-length comic book and called it *The Amazing Spider-Man*. It quickly became Marvel's most popular title. Spider-Man was popular with fans because he was more realistic than other superheroes. Peter Parker lived in New York City, not a fictional city like Superman's Metropolis. Spider-Man could not fly or turn invisible. Instead he relied on his homemade web shooter and acrobatic abilities to battle his enemies. More than anything, Parker and Spider-Man were vulnerable, whether it was getting picked on at school or losing a fight against the Green Goblin. But it was at these moments, when readers least expected it, that Lee masterfully used humor to entertain fans. When Spider-Man faced certain defeat, he often playfully mocked his villain, which relieved the tension of the situation. Humor in superhero comic books had never been used so freely or effectively before Lee used it with Spider-Man.

Lee continued his trendsetting ways by writing directly to readers in his captions. These unique captions reminded readers of action that had taken place an is-

The Amazing Spider-Man was an immediate success when it was published in 1963.

sue or two earlier or praised them for their detailed knowledge of the story. Lee's captions gave his stories a personal touch, but they also served another purpose: Because readers felt like they were a part of the story, they were more likely to return to the newsstand the next month to pick up the latest issue. This was critical in developing a fan base in the early days of Marvel Comics.

With Lee at the helm, Marvel Comics was publishing *The Fantastic Four*, *The Incredible Hulk*, *The Amazing Spider-Man*, *The Uncanny X-Men*, and several

The first two comic books to feature Spider-Man are very valuable today.

others. It is for this reason that the period came to be known as the Marvel Age of Comics. But for all of Marvel Comics' success in the early to mid-1960s, troubles were looming for the company and its unofficial leader, Stan Lee.

Chapter Four

Marvel Movie Magic

I n the fall of 1968, Martin Goodman sold his publishing business to Perfect Film and Chemical Corporation, which later changed its name to Cadence Industries. Company executives realized Stan Lee was now the recognized face of Marvel Comics, so they signed him to a three-year contract and gave him a pay raise. Marvel Comics was placed in the company's magazine management division, which Martin Goodman still oversaw.

This was when the relationship between Lee and Goodman started to sour. Goodman wanted Cadence Industries to give his son Chip control of the company. Lee, however, wanted the same for himself. But it did not matter which man controlled Marvel Comics. Neither one could prevent the decline in comic book sales. In 1970 the company stopped producing new *X-Men* stories each month, printing only old stories. Lee was disappointed, but continued to devote himself to writing groundbreaking stories for Marvel's other comics.

Stan Lee poses with actors costumed as Wolverine, the Incredible Hulk, and Spider-Man at the opening of the Marvel Mania restaurant in 1997.

In a three-part story for *The Amazing Spider-Man*, he examined the dangers of drug use, a growing problem in the United States at the time. In the story, Peter Parker's best friend, Harry Osborne, becomes addicted to drugs and nearly dies. Eventually, with Parker's (and Spider-Man's) help, Osborne is able to beat the habit. The series was praised by fans and received positive press coverage for the way it exposed the dark side of drug use.

After the success of the 1978 movie *Superman*, Stan Lee worked to bring his Marvel characters to the big screen.

In 1972 Lee finally won his struggle with Martin Goodman when Cadence Industries named him publisher of the company. He immediately gave up the day-to-day responsibilities of writing and editing comic books. Lee's main role as publisher was to expand the company's comic book line and to sign television and movie deals featuring Marvel's popular characters. He frequently traveled the country giving lectures and promoting Marvel Comics. Even though Lee was no longer actively writing or editing comics, he continued to have some creative control over the style and content of the books. That was obvious from the first panel of all Marvel comic books. Before each title were the words "Stan Lee Presents."

Hollywood Disappointment

Lee had long considered leaving New York and settling on the West Coast to pursue a career in movie production. After the successful 1978 *Superman* movie, Marvel granted Lee's wish and sent him to Los Angeles in hopes of securing motion picture deals for the company. Lee quickly had dozens of projects in the works, including Broadway shows featuring the superheroes Captain America and Thor. He arranged live-action television shows for Daredevil and the Black Widow. He even began working on a big-budget stage production featuring Silver Surfer.

By the early 1980s, Lee's fortunes began to change. He succeeded in getting several cartoon shows featuring Marvel comic book characters on television, including *Spider-Man and His Amazing Friends, G.I. Joe*, and *Muppet Babies*. But he had a much harder time finding success on the big screen. The movies *Howard the Duck, The Punisher,* and *Captain America* failed miserably at the box office. Lee was disheartened and unsure of his next move.

Meanwhile, Marvel Comics was losing readers. By the end of the 1980s, Marvel's top-selling comic books were *Wolverine* and *Punisher,* two characters Lee had no part in creating. It seemed Marvel was moving on without its longtime leader.

Marvel Movie Magic

Lee's employment arrangement with Marvel Comics changed in 1994 when he signed a lifetime contract to do just a few promotional engagements a year. Two years later, Marvel declared bankruptcy and attempted to void Lee's lifetime contract. Lee hired a lawyer and sued Marvel for the rights to the superhero characters he had created. Because he had been under a work-for-hire agreement in those days, the court sided with Marvel.

But the lawsuit resulted in a new contract for Lee. Under the contract, Lee became the chairman **emeritus** of Marvel Entertainment in 1998, earning an annual salary of nearly $1 million. He also continued his promotional engagements at comic book conventions and gave speeches and interviews promoting Marvel Comics.

The new contract also entitled Lee to 10 percent of company profits from movies and television deals that featured Marvel Comics superheroes. A short time later, Marvel began a successful run of movies. In 1998 a movie based on the little-known Marvel character Blade was released in theaters and did surprisingly well. This led the way for other Marvel releases, including

The movie version of Marvel's *Howard the Duck* was a box-office failure.

the 2000 box-office hit *X-Men*. The movie's plot had little to do with any of the original X-Men comic books, but the characters were uniquely Lee's.

Marvel's biggest blockbuster came in the summer of 2002, when *Spider-Man* hit theaters and earned more than $400 million worldwide. Lee served as executive producer and helped with many of the creative decisions. This ensured that the movie closely followed the story of the original comic books. Lee even had a

cameo role in the movie, saving a young girl from falling debris. Since that time, Marvel Entertainment has released several more superhero movies starring comic book characters created by Lee, including *Dare-devil*, *X-2: X-Men United*, *The Incredible Hulk*, *Spider-Man 2*, and *The Fantastic Four*.

Stan Lee Media

Even though Lee was still officially an employee of Marvel in the late 1990s, he had been working on launching his own company for some time. Lee hoped to start a media group and he invested heavily in the

Actor Tobey Maguire played the title role in the blockbuster films *Spider-Man* and *Spider-Man 2*.

Today, Stan Lee is almost as famous as the characters he created.

Internet, because he saw cyberspace as a great place to introduce new comic book superheroes. In 2000 he introduced the Web site StanLee.net, where he began marketing his newest creations and projects. The site also featured brief cartoon clips and interactive superhero games. That year, he also started Stan Lee Media. Unlike his arrangement with Marvel, with his new company Lee owned exclusive rights to any new characters he developed. Unfortunately, when the Internet boom of the 1990s collapsed in late 2000, Stan Lee Media was forced to close. Never one to give up, however, Lee later created POW! Entertainment to generate television and movie deals for his non-Marvel concepts.

Today, Lee lives in Los Angeles with his wife, Joan. With his trademark tinted glasses and silver mustache and hair, he is almost as recognizable as the superheroes he created. The architect of the modern comic book shows no signs of slowing down. He writes his daily Spider-Man comic strip, which he has done since 1979, and he continues to promote movies and comic books for Marvel Comics. But he is still searching for the next great superhero that will one day take the world by storm. "I'm aware that there's got to be a time when I'm not going to be able to do this," he says. "But I hope that time is far off, because I'm really enjoying what I'm doing. Somewhere inside of this old body, there's a young guy trapped, trying to get out."[11]

Notes

Chapter 1: Stanley Lieber

1. Stan Lee and George Mair, *Excelsior! The Amazing Life of Stan Lee*. New York: Fireside, 2002, p. 5.
2. Quoted in "Comic Relief by Stan Lee," *Edutopia*, September 2005, p. 58.
3. Lee and Mair, *Excelsior! The Amazing Life of Stan Lee*, p. 15.
4. Quoted in Jordan Raphael and Tom Spurgeon, *Stan Lee and the Rise and Fall of the American Comic Book*. Chicago: Chicago Review Press, 2003, p. 7.

Chapter 2: Stanley Becomes Stan Lee

5. Quoted in Raphael and Spurgeon, *Stan Lee*, p. 20.
6. Quoted in "Stan Lee," Salon.com, August 17, 1999, archive.salon.com/people/bc/1999/08/17/lee.
7. Quoted in Raphael and Spurgeon, *Stan Lee*, p. 27.

Chapter 3: Spider-Mania

8. Lee and Mair, *Excelsior! The Amazing Life of Stan Lee*, p. 105.
9. Quoted in Larry King Live Weekend, "Stan Lee Takes Superheroes Online," CNN.com, July 8, 2000, http://edition.cnn.com/TRANSCRIPTS/0007/08/lklw.00.html.
10. Quoted in Larry King Live Weekend, "Stan Lee Takes Superheroes Online."

Chapter 4: Marvel Movie Magic

11. Lee and Mair, *Excelsior! The Amazing Life of Stan Lee*, p. 270.

Glossary

borough: A political division of New York City.

cameo: A brief appearance in a movie by a well-known person.

emeritus: Someone who is retired but is given the honorary title of the last position he or she held.

Great Depression: A period of great economic slow-down beginning in 1929 and lasting through the 1930s.

immigrants: People who move to a new country and take up residence.

playwright: A person who writes plays.

recorder: A small, flutelike wind instrument.

For Further Exploration

Books

Stan Lee, *Just Imagine Stan Lee's Superman.* New York: DC Comics, 2001. Stan Lee rewrites the origins of DC Comics' most famous superhero.

Stan Lee and John Buscema, *How to Draw Comics the Marvel Way.* New York: Fireside, 1984. Lee and longtime Marvel artist John Buscema show readers how to draw characters in the Marvel style.

Stan Lee, Jack Kirby, John Romita, and Steve Ditko, *Marvel Visionaries: Stan Lee.* New York: Marvel Comics, 2005. This book contains a collection of historic comic books written by Stan Lee, including his first superhero story, "Captain America Foils the Traitor's Revenge."

Web Sites

Amazing Spider-Man Cover Gallery (www.samruby. com/title.htm). Includes full-color cover shots of the many comic books in the eleven Spider-Man titles.

Marvel.com (www.marvel.com). The official Web site of Marvel Comics. Includes information about upcoming Marvel movies, games, downloads, and more.

Index

Picture Credits

About the Author

Raymond H. Miller is the author of more than 50 nonfiction books for children. He has written on a range of topics from U.S. presidents to Native Americans. He enjoys reading comic books, playing sports, and spending time outdoors with his wife and two daughters.